EDO

The Bini People
of the Benin
Kingdom

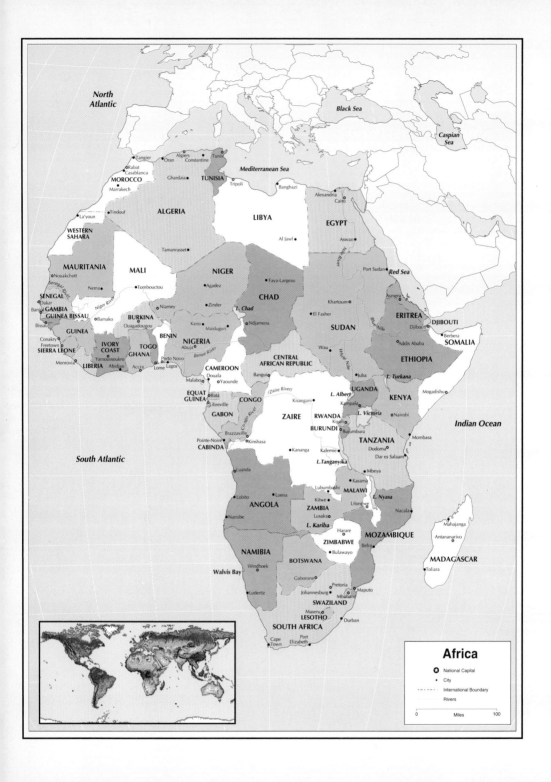

North
Atlantic

Black Sea

Caspian
Sea

Tangier
Rabat
Casablanca
MOROCCO
Marrakech

Algiers
Oran Constantine
Tunis
TUNISIA

Mediterranean Sea

Tripoli

Banghazi

Alexandria
Cairo

Ghardaia

La'youn
Tindouf

WESTERN
SAHARA

ALGERIA

LIBYA

EGYPT

Aswan

Al Jawf

Tamanrasset

MAURITANIA

Nouakchott

Nema

MALI

Tombouctou

NIGER

Agadez

Faya-Largeau

CHAD

Khartoum

Port Sudan

Red Sea

Asmera

ERITREA

DJIBOUTI

SENEGAL
Dakar
Banjul GAMBIA
GUINEA BISSAU
Bissau
GUINEA
Conakry
Freetown
SIERRA LEONE
Monrovia
LIBERIA

Niger River

Niamey

Zinder

L. Chad

Bamako

Ouagadougou

BURKINA

Kano

Maiduguri

Ndjamena

El Fasher

SUDAN

Blue Nile

Djibouti
Berbera
SOMALIA

Addis Ababa

IVORY
COAST
Yamoussoukro
Abidjan

TOGO
GHANA
Accra

BENIN

Abuja

NIGERIA

Benue River

CENTRAL
AFRICAN REPUBLIC

Bangui

Wau

White Nile

ETHIOPIA

Porto Novo
Lome Lagos

Malabo

CAMEROON

Douala
Yaounde

Juba

L. Turkana

UGANDA

Mogadishu

EQUAT.
GUINEA
Bata
Libreville

CONGO

GABON

ZAIRE

(Zaire River)

Kisangani

L. Albert

Kampala

RWANDA
Kigali
BURUNDI
Bujumbura

L. Victoria

Nairobi

KENYA

Mombasa

Indian Ocean

South Atlantic

Brazzaville

Pointe-Noire
Kinshasa
CABINDA

Kananga

Kalemie

TANZANIA

Dodoma

Dar es Salaam

L. Tanganyika

Luanda

Mbeya

Kasama

Lobito

Luena

ANGOLA

Lubumbashi

Kitwe

MALAWI

Lilongwe

L. Nyasa

Mahajanga

Namibe

ZAMBIA

Lusaka

Nacala

Antananarivo

L. Kariba

Harare

Walvis Bay

NAMIBIA

Windhoek

Luderitz

BOTSWANA

Gaborone

ZIMBABWE

Bulawayo

Belra

MOZAMBIQUE

MADAGASCAR

Toliara

Pretoria
Johannesburg
Mbabane
SWAZILAND
Maseru
LESOTHO
SOUTH AFRICA

Maputo

Durban

Cape
Town

Port
Elizabeth

Africa

⚹ National Capital
• City
--- International Boundary
Rivers

0   Miles   100

The Heritage Library of African Peoples

EDO

The Bini People of the Benin Kingdom

Chukwuma Azuonye, Ph.D.

THE ROSEN PUBLISHING GROUP, INC.
NEW YORK

Published in 1996 by The Rosen Publishing Group, Inc.
29 East 21st Street, New York, NY 10010

First Edition

Manufactured in the United States of America

Library of Congress Cataloging-in-Publication Data

Azuonye, Chukwuma, 1945–
    Edo : the Bini people of the Benin Kingdom / Chukwuma Azuonye.
      p. cm. — (The heritage library of African peoples)
    Includes bibliographical references and index.
    ISBN 0-8239-1985-4
    1. Bini (African people)—Juvenile literature. [1. Bini (African
people)] I. Title. II. Series.
DT515.45.B36A98   1995
966.9′3—dc20   94-38414
                                               CIP
                                               AC

Contents

INTRODUCTION

THERE IS EVERY REASON FOR US TO KNOW something about Africa and to understand its past and the way of life of its peoples. Africa is a rich continent that has for centuries provided the world with art, culture, labor, wealth, and natural resources. It has vast mineral deposits, fossil fuels, and commercial crops.

But perhaps most important is the fact that fossil evidence indicates that human beings originated in Africa. The earliest traces of human beings and their tools are almost two million years old. Their descendants have migrated throughout the world. To be human is to be of African descent.

The experiences of the peoples who stayed in Africa are as rich and as diverse as of those who established themselves elsewhere. This series of books describes their environment, their modes of subsistence, their relationships, and their customs and beliefs. The books present the variety of languages, histories, cultures, and religions that are to be found on the African continent. They demonstrate the historical linkages between African peoples and the way contemporary Africa has been affected by European colonial rule.

Africa is large, complex, and diverse. It encompasses an area of more than 11,700,000 square miles. The United States, Europe, and India could fit easily into it. The sheer size is an indication of the continent's great variety in geography, terrain, climate, flora, fauna, peoples, languages, and cultures.

Much of contemporary Africa has been shaped by European colonial rule, industrialization, urbanization, and the demands of a world economic system. For more than seventy years, large regions of Africa were ruled by Great Britain, France, Belgium, Portugal, and Spain. African peoples from various ethnic, linguistic, and cultural backgrounds were brought together to form colonial states.

For decades Africans struggled to gain their independence. It was not until after World War II that the colonial territories became independent African states. Today, almost all of Africa is ruled by Africans. Large numbers of Africans live in modern cities. Rural Africa is also being transformed, and yet its people still engage in many of their customs and beliefs.

Contemporary circumstances and natural events have not always been kind to ordinary Africans. Today, however, new popular social movements and technological innovations pose great promise for future development.

George C. Bond, Ph.D., Director
Institute of African Studies
Columbia University, New York

In the past and still today, the traditional king or Oba of Benin ruled in conjunction with many chiefs. This is Chief I. Obasoyen of Benin City, Nigeria.

chapter

1

THE PEOPLE AND THEIR LAND

THE NAMES BINI (PRONOUNCED *BEENEE*) AND
Benin (pronounced Beh*neen*) are of uncertain
origin. Benin was an ancient kingdom that
flourished for nearly one thousand years before
it was conquered by the British in 1897.

Today, the kingdom has been restored. Benin
City in Nigeria was, and remains, the center of
the rich traditions of Benin. The name of the
modern state of Benin (earlier called Dahomey)
honors the ancient kingdom of Benin but should
not be confused with the Benin kingdom or with
Benin City in Nigeria.

The kingdom of Benin was so extraordinary
and powerful that many of its neighbors still
refer to the Bini people with awe. However, the
Bini people have always called themselves Edo,
or Iduu, names that they also use for their land,
culture, and language.

The name Edo has come to be applied to

many neighboring languages, peoples, and cultures that are actually distinct and much closer to Yoruba. Yoruba and Edo are both, however, members of the Kwa group of languages that includes Igbo, Ewe in southern Ghana, and many other languages in the tropical rain forest regions stretching from Igbo territory to southern Liberia.

Edo oral traditions claim close connections to the neighboring Yoruba, particularly in the names and characteristics of the major deities in their religions. However, basic features of the Bini worldview and philosophy seem to be closer to the system of the neighboring Igbo in many respects.

The territory occupied by the kingdom of Benin, and still occupied by Edo today, lies in Edo State, Nigeria. It is low-lying land of porous soil called "Benin sand," crossed by several rivers and small streams. It is easily accessible by road from Lagos and also from Igboland and southeastern Nigeria. Good timber comes from the still unbroken rain forest and the timber reserves that cover more than 30 percent of the land. But recent economic trends show that agriculture and commerce are increasingly becoming more important than the exploitation of the forest resources.

Agricultural products are dominated by yams, cocoyams, cassava, maize, beans, rice, groundnuts, and vegetables. There are three distinct climatic seasons: the dry season (September to

The People and their Land

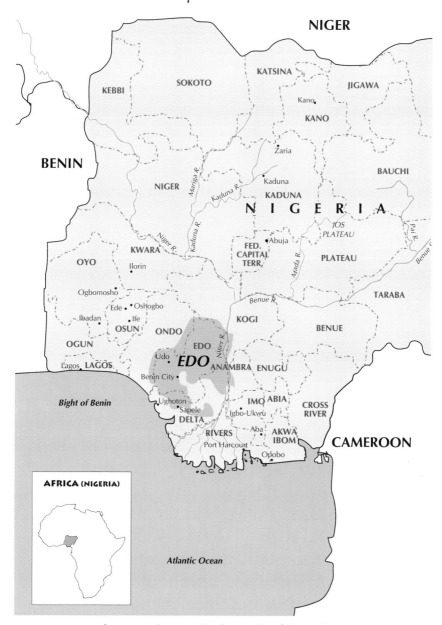

Map of Nigeria showing the location of the Edo people.

December); the Harmattan, characterized by a cold north wind that causes a caking of the soil (December to February); and the rainy season (March to early September). The planting cycle,

The Bini have preserved much of their traditional culture despite European influence as a result of colonialism. For example, the position of village chief or head is held, as it always has been, by the Enogie.

around late March, is marked by a division of labor. The men plant the men's crops (yams of various types), while the women plant the women's crops (maize and assorted vegetables). Intensive cultivation has contributed to the serious erosion problems.

Hunting and fishing are still very much part of the rural economy. The Edo are adept hunters, using both imported and homemade guns and traps. The most common game animals are bush-pigs and antelopes.

Many Edo are passionately committed to tradition. Despite Western influence, the major pillars of Edo culture survive. Support for the arts is a major social responsibility.▲

chapter

2

THE BENIN EMPIRE

THE KINGDOM OF BENIN IS BELIEVED TO HAVE come into being between 800 and 1000 AD. It probably began as a small city-state comprising what is now Benin City and the surrounding area. When Europeans arrived in 1485, the city was the capital of a vast empire. It appears to have covered much of present-day southern Nigeria, from Lagos and part of eastern Yorubaland to much of western Igbo country. Some Edo oral literature suggests that parts of northern Igbo, Anambra, Imo, Abia, and Rivers states were part of the Benin empire.

It also appears, however, that the rule of the Benin kings, or Obas, was strong only in the predominantly Edo areas and was resisted, sometimes violently, in the outer territories. Many believe that this was largely because the Igbo and other peoples were opposed to the type of one-man rule represented by the Obas of Benin. They had established a democratic form of government in which every man could aspire to become leader of his community through personal achievements.

▼ ORIGINS AND GROWTH OF THE EMPIRE ▼

The Edo have three major myths of origin in their oral traditions. First is a myth that the Edo or Iduu people have been on their land since the beginning of time. Second, some Edo claim to have migrated from the east. It is not clear, however, how far to the east their origins may have been. The third set of myths traces the origins of the institution of Oba and the ruling class to the city of Ife (*Uhe* in Edo), the cradle of Yoruba civilization.

Evidence suggests that all three origin accounts have some truth. The idea of always having been there may be true because southern Nigeria is one of the many centers in Africa in which the remains of ancient human beings have been unearthed. Settlements of stone-axe men (Achuleans) dating back 50,000 years have been discovered in present-day Abia state.

The myth of migration from Ife is clearly more recent. It is known that the first king of Benin was a Yoruba prince from Ife. Before that, however, Benin was ruled for centuries by kings who called themselves sky-kings, Ogiso (*ogie*,

THE STORY OF THE FIRST OBA

Although a foreigner, the first Oba, Oranmiyan, established himself securely in Benin. He set up the kingdom on the model of his native Ife kingdom and created hereditary chiefs called *onogie* to rule on his behalf in various parts of the kingdom. He seems to have gained the confidence of some groups by appointing their own leaders as chiefs, rather than sending Ife princes to rule directly over them.

Despite the success of this system, many Edo struggled for self-rule. In the end, Oranmiyan is said to have decided that only an Edo should rule the Edo. He therefore fathered a child with the daughter of an Edo chief and returned to Ife. That child, who is remembered in myths as Erinmwinde, was crowned Eweka I, beginning the Eweka Dynasty, which is still in existence.

king + *iso*, sky). Although the Ogiso were probably invaders, the Bini created myths to justify their conquest by linking them with the gods.

According to the most popular of these myths, the founder of the Benin kingdom was the youngest son of Osanobua, the supreme deity. At the beginning of historical time, Osanobua decided to send his children to live in the visible world (*agbon*). Among these were the first kings of Ife and other Yoruba kingdoms, and the first kings of the Europeans.

On departing from the invisible world (*erinmwin*), each son was permitted to take with him anything of value he wished. Whereas others chose wealth, magical power, and implements, on the advice of a bird the first king of Benin chose a snail shell. On their arrival in the world, the heavenly princes found it covered with water. Again on the advice of the bird, the Bini ancestor overturned the snail shell, whereupon sand poured out of it and spread to form the land. This, according to the myth, is how the Oba of Benin became the owner of the land. His brothers came to him to buy land with their possessions; thus he remains the wealthiest and most powerful ruler in the world.

▼ THE EWEKA DYNASTY ▼

The current Oba of Benin, Erediauwa I, is believed to be the 38th in the line of kings that goes back to Eweka I, who ruled between 1200 and 1300. The empire appears to have reached its zenith in the 1400s and 1500s. Its major achievements are the building of the city of Benin, the creation of organized armed forces and an efficient system of administration, the organization of guilds of artists and craftsmen

The Benin Empire

Benin continues to be ruled by a royal class. Pictured here are Princess Erediauwa, left, daughter-in-law of the current Oba, Erediauwa I, and one of his wives, below.

whose work became famous throughout the world, and the expansion of international trade (including, unfortunately, the slave trade).

In 1897, Benin City was sacked by the British. The kingdom and empire were taken over, and the ruling Oba was exiled. Although there was a restoration in 1914, the power of the Oba was greatly reduced and confined to Benin.

Oba Erediauwa I was trained as a lawyer at Oxford University. His major task has been to preserve the traditional features and role of the Benin monarchy while opening it up to the modern world.

▼ COLONIZATION AND DECLINE OF BENIN ▼

The decline and fall of the Benin empire was made possible by three major factors. First were the decay and corruption that set in within the kingdom at the height of its power. Second were the continual revolts within the kingdom and the resistance of the peoples it colonized. Third were the opening of the kingdom to European colonization through missionary activity, partnership in the slave trade, and finally the signing of a damaging treaty with the British.

The empire's first European contact began with the coming of the Portuguese (1485 to the 1660s), under whom Ughoton was established as a major seaport and trading post. Some European influence was established, but colonial

The people of Nigeria have battled oppression in some form since the late 15th century. Today, the Nigerian Army trains just outside of Lagos, the capital of Nigeria.

government was not set up over the rule of the Benin kings. The people of Benin developed great respect for Europeans and even came to see them as messengers of the sea god, Olokun. Worship of Olokun gained in strength.

During the Dutch phase (1600s to the late 19th century), Benin traded in slaves, leopard skins, pepper, and coral. Like the Portuguese before them, the Dutch did not try to set up a colonial government. The Benin empire expanded and contracted as its colonies revolted or were reconquered.

Late in the 19th century, the Dutch were gradually replaced by the British as Benin's main trading partner. It was during this phase that Benin was tricked into signing a treaty that eventually led to its fall to the British. The stage was set by the Oba, Adolo, who increased trade with the British. Adolo's son and successor, Ovonrramwen, who became king in 1888, stopped all trade with Europeans. But he was faced with many revolts among his subjects at the time. The British seized the opportunity to trick him into signing a treaty agreeing "to accept British protection, to refer disputes with traders and with other tribes to consular officials, to tolerate missionaries, and to allow his subjects to trade freely."

By the time Ovonrramwen realized his mistake, it was too late. He was a true believer in Benin traditions and independence, however, and it was impossible for him to observe the terms of an agreement that so dramatically reduced his power and the prestige of his kingdom. He went on to strengthen traditions and ceremonies that the British regarded as evil.

An attempt by the British to force a meeting with the Oba during a period of his ritual seclusion in 1897 led to the massacre by the Bini of the entire British mission in Benin City. In retaliation, the British attacked and sacked the city, looted its shrines and the Oba's palace of

The Edo retain much of their traditional ruling hierarchy. Chief Edogun of Benin City (above) and Queen Mother Aghahowa Niyoba of Uselu (below) both wear coral beads and have swords of office

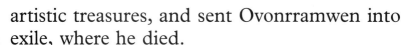

artistic treasures, and sent Ovonrramwen into exile, where he died.

Although the Benin monarchy was restored in 1914, it was no longer the center of a powerful empire. Its influence remained so great in some areas, however, that even in its reduced state some former subjects continued to pay tribute and to seek its judgment in local disputes, despite the presence of the British.

Nigeria won its independence in October 1960, and became a republic in October 1963. Although the country itself has since struggled between military rule and a civilian government, the Edo have basically managed to maintain rule over themselves.▲

chapter

3

SOCIAL LIFE AND CUSTOMS

THE SOCIAL LIFE, CUSTOMS, AND TRADITIONAL
life cycle of the Edo today are a legacy of the
system of authority that was developed in the
old Benin kingdom. In most of the empire, the
Oba was a distant figure. In many Edo village
communities, over which the Yoruba Oba was
not able to assert his power, leadership was ef-
fectively left in the hands of the oldest man,
odionwere, as was customary in the Edo system.

The fact that these two systems have existed
side by side over the years shows that the Yoruba
colonizers never fully established themselves as
the only source of power and authority in Benin.
Wherever native Edo resistance was overcome,
the Oba sent a client to rule as *onogie*, hereditary
chief. Today some village communities still
have two heads, an *onogie* (a representative of the
Oba) and an *odionwere* (a traditional headman).

People who live in small communities often know everyone in the village. The game these two boys are playing has become a social event.

A bronze plaque of an Oba on horseback, accompanied by retainers. Made in the 1600s when the Benin kingdom was powerful, such brass artworks are found in museums throughout the world. Many plaques decorate the Oba's palace in Benin City today.

Over the years, conflicts between the alien Oba and the indigenous Edo led to the emergence of a balance between the Oba's representatives on the one hand and representatives of the people (his potential opponents) on the other. This balance has been achieved by the introduction of nonhereditary chiefly orders into which any freeborn person can enter through hard work and personal achievement. In this way the Obas have, over the years, been able to broaden their hold on a wider range of native Edo peoples. Today, the prestige of belonging to these nonhereditary chiefly orders remains one of the few areas in which the modern Oba has continued to wield influence.

COMING OF A NEW OBA

The ceremonies surrounding the installation of a new Oba and the burial of the old are among the most elaborate and colorful forms of dramatic events. Recollections of actual events are mixed up with rituals enacting major myths. All are intended to repeat the claims of the Oba to rule.

Dozens of plays can be made out of one coronation event alone. The ceremonies last more than a year and fall into three stages. The first stage depicts the new Oba's youth and training by the priests and doctors. In the second stage he performs the funeral rites for his late father. In this way he lays claim to succession. In the final stage the new Oba goes through a journey of several centuries, beginning at the gateway to the land of spirits, through important landmarks in history, and ending in Benin City, where he is crowned. The most important parts of his journey are those that dramatize the beginnings of his links with the gods and the creation of the Bini people.

▼ THE LAYOUT OF BENIN CITY ▼

As with the division between the Oba and the indigenous people, the city of Benin is divided into two major sectors, the palace (*ogbe*) and the town (*ore*). Today, the two sectors are divided by a road; in the past there was an inner city wall. The palace is the home of the Oba, his wives and children, the kingmakers (*Uzama*), and the palace chiefs. Both the palace and the town are divided into wards. In the palace itself, each ward is divided into apartments (*ugha*); each department is a living space, a store, a workshop, or an arena for public ceremonies. Others serve as reception halls or as shrines or altars to deceased Oba. All apartments, especially those dedicated for rituals and public receptions, are lavishly decorated with bronze or brass plaques, pennants, carved pillars, and a wide variety of ornate furniture and decorative objects.

▼ AGE GRADES ▼

Outside of the complex form of administration in Benin City, the Edo age-based system continues to be the main form of social organization in outlying areas. This system grades all members of each community according to age. The lowest age grade, *iroghae*, comprises boys between the ages of 15 and 20. Its members undertake such minor projects as clearing the paths to streams and farms and repairing shrines and other communal buildings.

The next age grade, the *ighele*, serve as police officers and soldiers. The highest age grade, the *edio* (singular, *odio*), comprises the elders of the community; they serve as village legislators and judges. The head of the community, *odionwere*, is

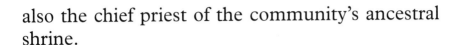
also the chief priest of the community's ancestral shrine.

▼ THE FAMILY ▼

Edo society has four types of family: nuclear, polygamous, joint, and extended. The nuclear family comprises a man, one wife, and their children. Traditionally, this was a poor man's family; farming required more working members. The polygamous family—a man, two or more wives, and their children—is still the vogue among wealthy traditionalists.

The joint family comprises an elderly man, his wife or wives, and the families (nuclear, polygamous, or both) of his grown sons. The old man is accepted as the head of the family and father of all its members. The joint family may arise out of economic or social need. In some cases, however, the joint family may be created by default when two or more of a man's sons remain in his house and raise children.

The extended family comprises several nuclear, polygamous, and joint families, who live in adjoining compounds but consider themselves one family. The great-grandfather, the grandfather, or his most senior son is head of the family.

In all types of families, leadership is based on age and masculinity. The oldest male member inherits all property and titles, and his relation-

A shrine in Benin City combines many sacred objects, including sculptures, stones, and cloth.

ship with his dependents is master-servant. His decisions are unquestioned, but he is expected to rule with fairness and wisdom. As living counterpart of the family's ancestors, he is chief priest of its ancestral shrines and its representative in the community *edio*.

This male-centered system, however, is in no respect male chauvinism. Women are not only highly visible in Bini society but are often partners in farming, trading, religious rites, and professional practices such as medicine.

In general, the family is the primary center of religious activity. In addition to the ancestral shrine, most families have shrines for various deities and spirits. The head of the family is also the family's chief priest.▲

29

chapter

4

WORLDVIEW AND RELIGION

IN EDO PHILOSOPHY, THE UNIVERSE IS DIVIDED into the visible world, *agbon*, and the invisible world, *erinmwin*. This view affects every aspect of the religion, art, and daily life of the people. It should also be noted that Edo traditions were brought to the Americas and the Caribbean during the days of slavery, so many Edo traditions thrive today in these parts of the world.

▼ THE VISIBLE WORLD: *AGBON* ▼

The visible world is seen as a mass of earth completely surrounded by limitless water. Into this vast expanse of water flow all the rivers of the earth. Besides human beings and other animals, *agbon* is the home of good and evil deities and spirits. The deities are believed to be children of the supreme god, Osanobua, who were sent down to live among humankind at the

A shrine to the Supreme God in the palace of Chief Ogiamwen, where the Chief worships every *eken* day, the fourth day of the traditional Edo four-day week.

beginning of time. They include the earth goddess, Obiemwen, creator of the earth; the water deity, Olokun, who today is more prominent as the god of wealth, fertility, and creativity; and the deity of death, Ogiuwu, whose worship is no longer prominent. Others are Oshun, the god of medicine, and Ogun, the god of metals.

▼ THE INVISIBLE WORLD: *ERINMWIN* ▼

All that is known of the world beyond is that it lies somewhere beyond the waters. It is spoken

of as heaven, as "worldunder," and as the world
across the seas. It is the home of the supreme
god, Osanobua, and of a group of spirits called
ehi, the personal guardian spirits of human
beings. With Osanobua, the *ehi* control human
destinies. Also residing in *erinmwin* are the spirits of the dead fathers of individuals (*arha*) and
the unnamed dead fathers of the community as
a whole (*edion*). These ancestral spirits are
worshiped by their living descendants in *agbon*
and are still seen as heads of their families and
contributors to their well-being in various ways.
Any family member who fails to meet his duties
is immediately punished by the ancestors. As a
reminder of this authority, each spirit is represented in the ancestral shrine by carved wood or
ivory staves in the shape of whips called *ukhurue*.

▼ FORCES IN THE UNIVERSE ▼

Each of the two worlds of the Edo, *erinmwin*
and *agbon*, is a system of good and evil forces,
each seeking control. Similarly, humans are
made up of powerful forces of good and evil,
each acting against the other.

Both forces are found in every part of the
body, but their greatest points of concentration
are in the head (*uhunmwun*), the seat of knowledge, and the hand (*obo*), the seat of action.
Thus, there are evil animals, humans, spirits,
and deities as well as helpful ones. The main

This bronze plaque depicts the entrance to the palace of the Oba of Benin. The entrance is adorned with a python, king of snakes and messenger of the water deity Olokun. The door is flanked by two attendants on each side.

focus of Edo religion and rituals is to strengthen human ties with the good forces and ward off the evil.

▼ LIFE CYCLES ▼

According to Edo belief, every human being has fourteen opportunities to be born again into *agbon*. Thereafter the individual settles permanently in *erinmwin* as an ancestor or hero-deity, depending on the degree of success achieved in previous reincarnations. Edo religion and rituals suggest that the goal of the human being in every lifetime is to achieve material success, to attain ripe old age, and to be recognized as having lived a worthy life. Such a life assures the opportunity of reincarnation and of eventually becoming an ancestor. At the beginning of each life cycle, the spirit kneels before Osanobua and declares what it intends to do in the world. When these wishes are sealed by Osanobua, they become the individual's destiny and cannot be changed for that life cycle.

▼ RELIGION AND RITUALS OF DAILY LIFE ▼

Edo religion and rituals focus on controlling the evil forces that work against human interests and ensuring the increase of the good forces. Since both categories exist both within and outside the individual, the rituals include personal and communal types.

Osanobua, the supreme deity, is naturally first among the good forces. Although he is commonly portrayed in myths and art as a great Oba living in splendor in *erinmwin,* most Edo tend to see him more as an invisible force that holds the universe in balance.

In its traditional form, the worship of Osanobua consists simply of raising a small mound of earth as a shrine and inserting into it a stick bearing a white cloth or flag. Blood sacrifice is rare in the worship of Osanobua. The most common offerings are colanuts, chalk, and fluted gourds.

Of the lower deities, the most powerful was traditionally Obiemwen, who supervised the fertility of the earth. Today, Obiemwen has been reduced to a deity of childbirth and is somewhat overshadowed by Olokun.

Olokun was originally the deity of the waters surrounding the visible world. Today, he is associated with water in many more ways. As the lord of the water between the two worlds through which all must pass at birth, he is worshiped as the bringer of children. Olokun is also associated with wealth. His worship is found at every level of the society, from the family to the kingdom. Goats are commonly sacrificed. Vigorous dancing is held, during which women worshipers desiring children and artists seeking creative power go into trance. In

Bini boys awaiting an initiation ceremony for the Olokun religious group.

an annual festival, new mothers and fulfilled artists give thanks to Olokun.

Two other major gods, Ogun and Oshun, are both good and evil. Of the purely evil gods, Ogiuwu and Eziza are the most prominent. Oshun, the god of medicine, is associated with the healing powers hidden in the leaves, bark, and roots of trees in the forest. His image is never pictured in human form. He is associated with vultures and chameleons, and images of these animals are found in carved objects around his shrines and in the iron staffs, *osun emator*, of doctors and priests.

Ogun is the power that is believed to be present in all types of metal. Farming imple-

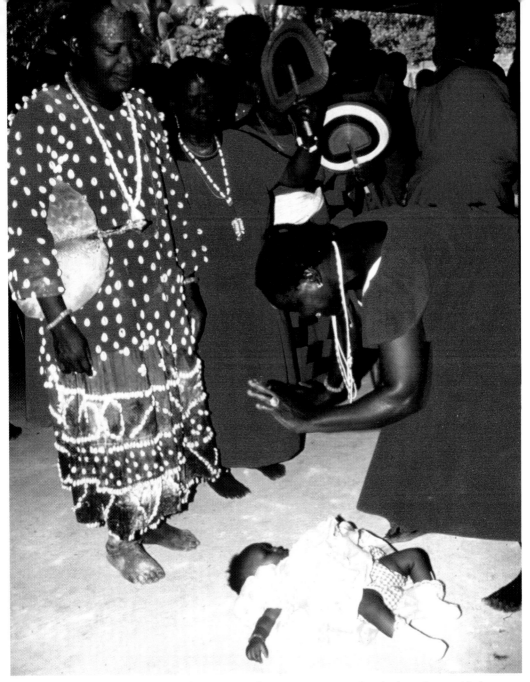

An important deity among the Edo is Shango, associated with thunder and lightning. He is also worshiped by the Yoruba people of Nigeria and by many people of African descent in the Americas. Here Shango followers bless a child in Benin City.

ments, guns, and all products of blacksmiths and—in recent years—of modern factories, including automobiles, trains, and airplanes, contain the power of Ogun. The major sign of Ogun is a miniature hammer and tongs, and his shrines comprise large piles of scrap metal. Almost all households have Ogun shrines of their own, but the deity is strongest among those who use metal in their work, especially hunters, metalsmiths, farmers, soldiers, and, today, drivers of vehicles of all kinds. Ogun is seen as a hot-tempered power who can do harm when least expected. This is no doubt a mythical way of stating known facts about use of metals. Ogun is commonly represented in human form, usually in the form of one of his special followers. Sacrificial offerings are made in the form of dog meat, tortoise, snail, and palm oil.

Although Ogiuwu has become less important today, this ancient god is still remembered as a great force for evil who is sometimes seen as the Bini equivalent of Satan.

▼ SERVING THE SPIRIT FORCES ▼

The Edo make a distinction between two types of ancestors: the named individual ancestors of families (*erha*), and the unnamed collective ancestors of the larger community (*edio*). The worship of the *erha* is an everyday domestic affair, whereas the worship of the *edio* is impor-

Many Bini ceremonies focus on ensuring that evil forces are kept from harming humans. This masked dancer, *Ighogho*, wards off smallpox and other dangerous diseases.

tant on major ceremonial occasions and festivals
at the village and higher levels of the society.

Sacrifices to the *erha* are required as soon as
it is known that the wife is pregnant. Naming
ceremonies include sacrifices to both family
and community ancestors. In the village age-
grade system, promotion from one grade to the
next calls for sacrifices and prayers to the community ancestors. The finale of every funeral
ceremony of the head of a family is *ukove*
(planting), during which carved wood or ivory
ukhurue staves are placed in an altar dedicated
to him, representing a new addition to the tem-
ple of family ancestors. The sacrifice of a goat
follows.

A wide variety of evil spirits associated with
nature must be averted through rites and sacrifices. Among them are Eziza, spirit of the whirl-
wind; Eseku, dwarfs that haunt lonely places to
seize and harm passersby, especially children;
Adabi, spirit of the crossroads (Igha-ede) which
is seen as the meeting point of good and evil
forces; Einwaren-ason, the elders of the night;
and Ighele-Erinmwin, founding fathers of the
underworld who are pictured as monsters that
snatch people away.

▼ SERVING THE HUMAN FORCES ▼

For Edo who follow traditional religion, the
most important forces that individuals seek to

control are those associated with the head, the hand, and the personal guardian spirit.

The head (*uhunmwun*), the seat of knowledge and reasoning, is a powerhouse of forces that are vital for the survival of the individual in *agbon*. Those forces do not always work in human interests. Edo speak of some persons as having a "good head" and others as having a "bad head." Every effort must be made to ensure that the head works in the interests of the person. The ritual of "serving the head" is a way of ensuring that one is able to control and reinforce the life forces that reside in the head. At the end of every year, everyone performs offerings to his head (*igue*) in his home and also participates in the communal Igue festival for the renewal of the Edo people as a whole.

Closely associated is the cult of service to one's personal guardian spirit (*ehi*). Although the *ehi* lives in the spirit world, its power is felt in the daily life of every person through the head. Reasoning, thinking, and decision-making are all affected by the power of the *ehi*.

The ritual of "serving the hand" (*ikengobo*) is associated with honest work that leads to solid personal achievement. The ritual makes a distinction between the right or good hand and the left or evil hand. It is carried out before and after a person undertakes a major venture, to ensure that only the positive forces of the right hand are released. Most homes have altars of the hand in the form of an elephant trunk ending in a hand holding a leaf or branch.

All human beings act on one another in different ways, positive and negative. Family generally can be counted upon to be helpful; other human beings carry evil forces. The Oba is revered as a deity whose health and actions have a direct effect on the destiny of the nation. Minor rulers are believed to possess similar powers to a lesser degree. By the same token, village headmen (*odionwere*) and heads of families embody forces in their own domains.

Since their arrival in the 1400s, Europeans have been represented among the Edo and in the art of Benin as carriers of potentially harmful forces as well as bringers of wealth. Coming as they did from across the sea, they were indentified with Olokun, the water god. It was from this time that the growth of Olokun worship began to increase, as overseas trade and prosperity were associated with the water god and the Europeans as his messengers. Today, Europeans occupy a major place in Edo mythology. In magical practice, the body parts of European people are regarded as containing powerful forces. Thus their hair and nails are sold as charms in traditional medicine shops.

Other human carriers of powerful forces are the doctors (*ibo*; singular, *obo*). Seen as carriers

This figure of an armed Portuguese soldier reflects the belief of the Bini that Europeans were carriers of potentially harmful forces.

of both evil and good forces, *ibo* may do good or evil depending on their calling. But since the great majority of *ibo* apply their powers against evil forces, they may be considered controllers of evil forces. Of these the most common are herb and root doctors (*obodi*); bone doctors (*uxegie*); crossroads doctors (*obo n'ighaede*), who control the power of witches and evil spirits; and forensic doctors (*obita*), who use various types of ordeals to detect guilt. For instance, suspects may be made to pick tiny seeds from hot oil, to withstand the passing of a feather through their tongue, or to survive the drinking of poisonous broths to prove innocence.

Another category of *ibo* are diviners, who use their powers to establish links between human beings and the helpful powers of the spirit world. Edo diviners practice four types of divination. Of these, the most ancient is *ogwega*, in which the diviner throws four strings of four shells each. The pattern of convex and concave figures made by each throw is interpreted to advise the client. The second and third types are very similar to *ogwega*. The fourth type, *iwawa*, is a complex system of numbers and signs. The diviner casts several small figures of humans, animals, and objects. Their relative positions are then interpreted and used to advise the client.

In addition to protecting clients from illness and misfortune, an important function of Bini doctors and diviners is to guard against the ever-present action of witches. Witches are called *azen*, a name that links them to the forces of darkness. It is believed that they have strong contacts with the evil gods and spirits and are frequently possessed by these evil forces. Although witches operate mainly at night, their action can be felt at any time in lonely spots, especially at crossroads—where sacrifices or traps are commonly placed for them.

▼ ANIMALS AND PLANTS AS FORCES ▼
IN BINI RITUAL

Like human beings, animals are seen as bearers of either good or evil forces. Many are believed to possess magical powers. Thus, women with a tendency to miscarry may be given a potion of freshwater snail to eat "to cool things down," or one containing spider "to bind the fetus in the womb." For hiccups, a potion is given containing pygmy kingfisher, a bird whose head bobs like one suffering from hiccups. Vultures and related types of birds are generally seen as messengers of death or disaster, as is the white-tailed ant thrush, called the bird of prophecy for its harsh cry.

By contrast certain animals are associated with good luck and the power to acquire wealth. The horned puff adder is quick and highly accurate in snapping at its prey with its long curved

Red coral is highly valued because it contains spiritual power (ase) from the water god Olokun. This chief wears coral beads for his initiation in Benin City.

fangs. Snakes, especially the most dangerous, are associated with Oshun, god of medicine, and therefore with the power to overcome harmful forces.

A number of animals are admired for their beauty, their dignity, or their speed, notably the leopard, the python, and the Nile crocodile.

Other animals represent harmful forces, especially the elephant, which is the prime symbol of the destructive forces of opposition.

Some animal parts, like certain human parts, are particularly valued. The beak of the white-backed vulture is used in the *ewawa* system of divination described above. The red tail feathers of the parrot are believed to shield the wearer against hostile forces. The feathers of the fish eagle are associated with the attainment of high status. Already mentioned is the trunk-hand, a positive symbol that represents the ability to gather wealth—just as the elephant uses its trunk to gather leaves and other objects. More generally, the trunk-hand represents the power to crash through obstacles and take whatever one needs.

Evil and good forces are believed to be contained in various inanimate objects, especially coral beads. Red coral is particularly valued because it is believed to contain spiritual power (*ase*) from the water god Olokun. Also connected with Olokun are mirrors and other reflectors, which have become powerful symbols.▲

chapter

5

THE ARTS AND
TECHNOLOGY

AMONG THE EDO, ALL ART IS SEEN AS AN
imitation of the act of creation by which
Osanobua created the world and the beings in it.
Artists are therefore like god when they create,
and they create under inspiration from the gods.
The artist receives the power of creation (*ase*) in
dreams and visions, usually after much suffering.
In some cases a person is revealed as an artist
through divination or through possession. But at
some stage, the artist is directly instructed by
Olokun on the creation of things with materials
found in the visible world.

Edo artists fall into two categories. The traditional artists see their works purely as service to
religion and celebration of the history of Benin.
They usually work in secrecy, using traditional
tools and techniques. Modern artists create for

An Edo bronze caster models wax over clay figures.

the general public, working openly in modern workshops with modern tools.

Like farm work and other Edo activities, art forms created by men and by women tend to differ. Male artists use hard materials such as wood, ivory, and metals, whereas female artists prefer clay, skins, gourds, and textiles.

▼ ARTISTS GUILDS ▼

The *Iwebo* association is responsible for maintaining the art and regalia of the Oba. Affiliated with it are guilds of specialized artists. Each guild lives in a different ward of the town. The

49

most prominent are the guild of bronze casters (*Iguneronmwon*) and the guild of carvers in wood and ivory (*Igbesanmwan*). Others include the carpenters' guild (*Onwina*), the weavers' guild (*Onwina n'Edo*), and others responsible for pottery, blacksmithing, and other arts and technology associated with the Oba and the palace. The Oba's pages and sword-bearers (*Emada*, sing., *Omada*) have long been associated with special wood-carving skills, especially for carving finely decorated stools, *agba*, used in royal ceremonies, as well as a wide variety of objects from household furniture to decorated bowls.

▼ THE BENIN BRONZES ▼

The best preserved examples of early art are in bronze (an alloy of copper and zinc) or brass (copper and tin). The most famous of the bronzes include masks, portraits of various Oba, and historical plaques. It is likely that the faces in some of the masks are actual portraits of Obas of the past.

It is not known when and how bronze-casting began in Benin. In general, the "lost wax" technique appears to have been common. In this technique, a wax model of the object is covered with clay. The wax is then melted and drained from the clay mold, into which molten brass or bronze is poured.

Some of the most famous bronze castings are of past kings and queens. This bronze is of a Queen Mother of the 16th century. Her hairstyle and neck are shown as covered in coral beads.

Today, the casting tradition continues to flourish. It fulfills both local needs and the demand for bronze sculptures from international collectors. Other arts from Benin also continue in this way.

▼ CARVINGS ▼

Benin is famous for its beautiful carved ivory horns, gongs, and masks. Among the best known are the Afro-Portuguese ivories, ordered from Bini artists by Portuguese navigators in the 1400s and 1500s. Among them are elaborate spoons, combs, salt-cellars, dagger handles, and hunting horns.

A few beautifully decorated objects in wood from this time still exist but are not well preserved.

Weaving and interior decoration were also well-developed artistic forms.

▼ LITERATURE ▼

Among the Edo, traditional tales (*oxa*) include those told as true and those told purely for entertainment. The tales told as true are largely in the form of myths about the origins of things and the beliefs and rituals of the people. Other "true" tales are legends celebrating the doings of heroes and rulers.

Edo poetry consists of songs (*ihuan*). These,

Many aspects of Edo art and culture have been passed on through the centuries. Here Okao Awerioghene, a woman of rank, wears coral beads like those shown in old Benin bronzes.

with proverbs and riddles, form part of *ibota*, the passing on of history within the family. They have been kept alive through the centuries.▲

53

chapter

6

THE EDO TODAY

THE EDO TODAY ARE STILL A PREDOMINANTLY rural people. Most live in villages that range in size from a few dozen to a few thousand people, and they continue to farm the land.

If a farm family is in need of something, or has something in surplus, it is time to visit the local market. Every village has its own market, or if it is small, shares one with a neighboring village. The rural markets operate every four days, while the town markets are open every other day. In the markets a vast array of items are bought and sold, from basic foods such as corn and plantains, to fabric for clothing and goods from other parts of Africa and overseas. But the markets serve other purposes as well. They provide an occasion for the rural Edo to exchange news and other information. In this way the markets are like the newspapers and the

Many different kinds of food and supplies are available at the local market.

radio and television stations available in the towns. Since market days occur regularly, the rural Edo reckon time by them. Each market day marks the start of a four-day "week." Moreover, market days are especially set aside for religious observances, including offerings to the gods and ancestors.

Those Edo who are not farmers live in towns and cities. The principal city of the Edo is still Benin City, as it has been for centuries. Well known for its long and colorful history, it has now become a thoroughly modern city, renowned in Nigeria for its cleanliness and the quality of its roads. The city, with a population

55

In Africa babies are generally carried on their mothers' backs. These young Edo girls both carry dolls in this way.

of about 250,000, is a cultural and artistic center in Nigeria. It boasts the University of Benin (established in 1970) and a national museum. It is also the capital of Edo State.

Benin City remains the home of the Oba, his court, and his noblemen. Many members of the nobility are wealthy and own businesses that provide work for their fellow city-dwellers. Some, for instance, harvest cash crops (like rubber and cocoa) from large plantations outside of town. Others own parts of the rain forest and cut down trees for timber. They then sell the rubber, cocoa, and timber abroad through export firms. Men and women of Benin City work in the offices of such companies. Many young Edo travel to the larger city of Lagos, hoping to find an even more vibrant business environment.

Benin City is still the home of the ancient craft guilds. The craft techniques tend to be passed along through the generations of a family.

As the capital of Edo State, Benin City is the home of the state government. Many Edo find work in the civil service for Edo State. Local government authorities are found in the other Edo towns, so people there find civil service work as well.

Benin City and the smaller towns contain a number of schools. Men and women are employed as teachers and administrators in these

Many Edo start their own businesses in towns and cities in Nigeria. This man is a professional sign painter in Benin City.

schools. In this way, the Edo participate in Nigeria's drive toward improved education and literacy.

Edo State was carved by the Nigerian government out of Bendel State in 1993. This marked the first time in Nigeria's then 30-year history that the Edo, along with their neighbors and close kinsmen, had their own state. This new status intensifies the challenges faced by the Edo as one of the many peoples of Nigeria. They, like the others, must follow a social and political program that works toward improvement of their people. In doing so, they face the conflict between modernization and the preservation of the

Chiefs, such as Chief Ize Iyamu of Benin City seen here,
continue Benin's rich tradition of local rulers.

essential principles of their culture. Moreover,
the progress of the Edo must occur in concert
with the progress of the other peoples, and of
Nigeria as a whole.

The Edo are learning from the triumphs and
failures of their past. They are confidently and
proudly using this knowledge to write new chapters of Edo history today.▲

Glossary

agbon Visible world.

ase Spiritual power.

azen Witches.

edio Highest age grade; village legislature.

ehi Personal guardian spirit.

erinmwin Invisible world.

ibo Doctors and diviners.

ibota Oral history.

Igha-ede Crossroads, symbol of meeting of good and evil.

ighele Middle age grade.

iroghae Lowest age grade.

Kwa African language family.

Obiemwen Earth goddess.

Oba King or emperor of Benin.

obo The hand, seat of action.

odionwere Oldest man in the community.

Ogiso Sky king.

Ogun God of metal.

ogwega Method of divination.

Olokun Water deity.

onogie Hereditary chief.

Osanobua Supreme deity.

oswa emator Staff of doctors and priests.

oxa Traditional tales.

uhunmwun The head, the seat of knowledge.

60

For Further Reading

Ben-Amos, Dan. *Sweet Words: Story-Telling Events in Benin*. Philadelphia: Center for the Study of Human Issues, 1975.

Ben-Amos, Paula. *The Art of Benin*. London: Thames and Hudson, 1980.

Ben-Amos, Paula, and Rubin, Arnold, (eds.). *The Art of Power, The Power of Art: Studies in Benin Iconography*. Los Angeles: UCLA Museum of Cultural History. Monograph Series No. 19. 1983.

Galembo, Phyllis. *Divine Inspiration*. Albuquerque: University of New Mexico Press, 1993.

Roth, Henry Ling. *Great Benin*, 1903. Reprinted New York: Barnes & Noble, 1968.

Ryder, A. *Benin and the Europeans, 1485–1897*. New York: Humanities Press, 1969.

Index

ABOUT THE AUTHOR
Currently Chair of the Department of Africana Studies at
the University of Massachusetts, Boston, Chukwuma
Azuonye earned a B.A. *summa cum laude* in English litera-
ture at the University of Nigeria, Nsukka, and a Ph.D. in
African literature from the School of Oriental and African
Studies, University of London. A specialist in African oral
literature, he has taught in three Nigerian universities
(Ibadan, Nsukka, and Lagos) and was acting Chair of the De-

partment of Linguistics and Nigerian Languages at the University of Nigeria, Nsukka (1986–88). In 1988–89 he participated in founding the Center for Igbo Studies at the Imo State University, Okigwe, and he held a Fulbright Senior Fellowship in the Department of Folklore and Folklife, University of Pennsylvania (1991–92). The founding editor of several scholarly and cultural journals, he introduced a new generation of Nigerian poets through the now-vintage anthology, *Nsukka Harvest* (1972). His poetry, short stories, and numerous scholarly papers and monographs have been published in journals in Africa, Europe, and the Americas.

CONSULTING EDITOR
Gary N. Van Wyk, Ph.D.

PHOTO CREDITS
Cover, pp. 8, 12, 17, 21, 24, 29, 36, 37, 46, 53, 55, 56, 58, 59 by Phyllis Galembo; pp. 19, 39, 49 © Eliot Elisofon/National Museum of African Arts, Eliot Elisofon Photographic Archives, Smithsonian Institution; p. 33 © Werner Forman Archive/Art Resource, Museum für Völkerkunde, Berlin; p. 51 © Werner Forman Archive/Art Resource, Museum of Mankind, London; p. 25 © Werner Forman Archive/Art Resources, British Museum, London; p. 31 © Werner Forman Archive/Art Resource, London/New York; p. 43 © Art Resource/The Bridgeman Art Library, British Museum, London.

DESIGN
Kim Sonsky